learn to draw
Rainforest & Jungle Animals

Learn to draw and color 21 different exotic creatures, step by easy step, shape by simple shape!

Illustrated by Robbin Cuddy
Written by Sandy Phan

Associate Publisher: Rebecca J. Razo
Art Director: Shelley Baugh
Project Manager: Amanda Weston
Associate Editor: Stephanie Meissner
Production Artists: Debbie Aiken, Amanda Tannen
Production Manager: Nicole Szawlowski
Production Coordinator: Lawrence Marquez
Production Assistant: Kate Davidson

Illustrated by Robbin Cuddy
Written by Sandy Phan

www.walterfoster.com
Walter Foster Publishing, Inc.
3 Wrigley, Suite A
Irvine, CA 92618

1 3 5 7 9 10 8 6 4 2

Table of Contents

Getting Started

When you look closely at the drawings in this book, you'll notice that they're made up of basic shapes, such as circles, ovals, and triangles. To draw all your favorite creatures, just start with simple shapes as you see here. It's easy and fun!

Circles are the base of this scarlet macaw's head and eye.

Ovals are good for drawing a gorilla's body and head.

Triangles are perfect for drawing ears like the ones on this leopard.

Tools & Materials

Before you begin, gather some drawing tools, such as paper, a regular pencil, an eraser, and a pencil sharpener. For color, you can use markers, colored pencils, paint, crayons, or even colored chalk.

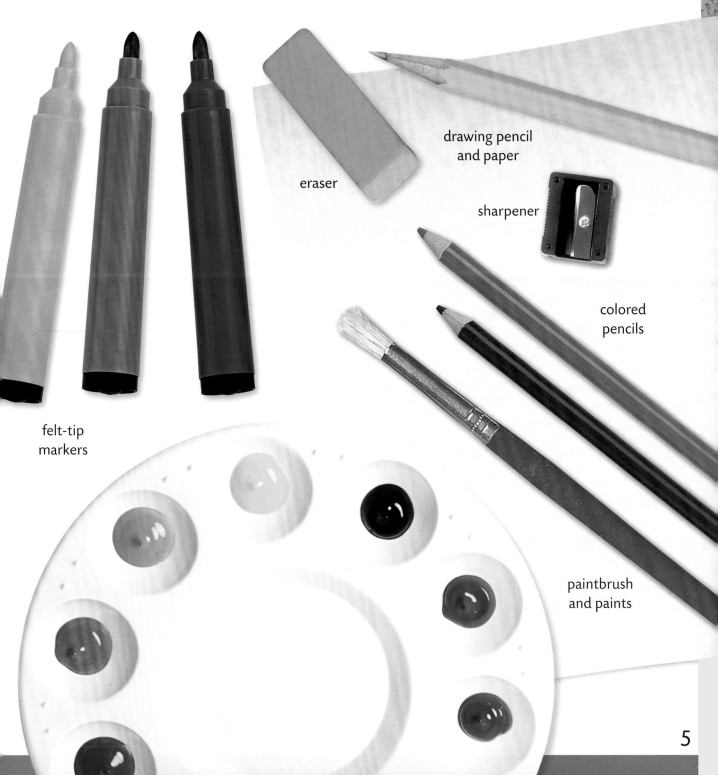

eraser

drawing pencil and paper

sharpener

colored pencils

felt-tip markers

paintbrush and paints

Gorilla

This gentle giant has a cone-shaped head, and its arms are longer than its legs. It loves to eat and nap all day!

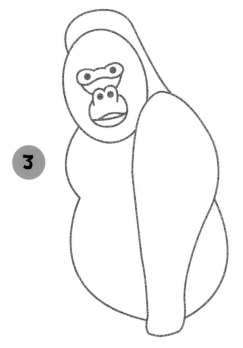

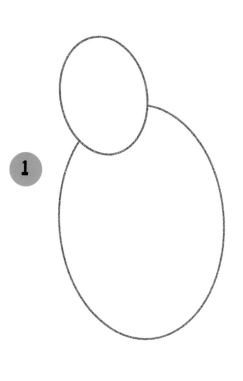

6

5

At Risk

Gorillas are **endangered**, or at risk of dying out. Humans are cutting down trees and taking over the land gorillas live on. Some hunters kill gorillas for bushmeat. These apes also catch deadly diseases like ebola.

6

fun fact

Gorillas are the largest **primates**, a group of animals that includes other apes and humans. Like humans, each gorilla has a different set of fingerprints. Gorillas can also stand on two legs, but they like to knuckle walk on their curled fingers and feet. Gorillas are very smart, and some have been taught to use sign language!

Jaguar

Jaguars are large wild cats. Most have tan or orange-brown fur with black spots called "rosettes."

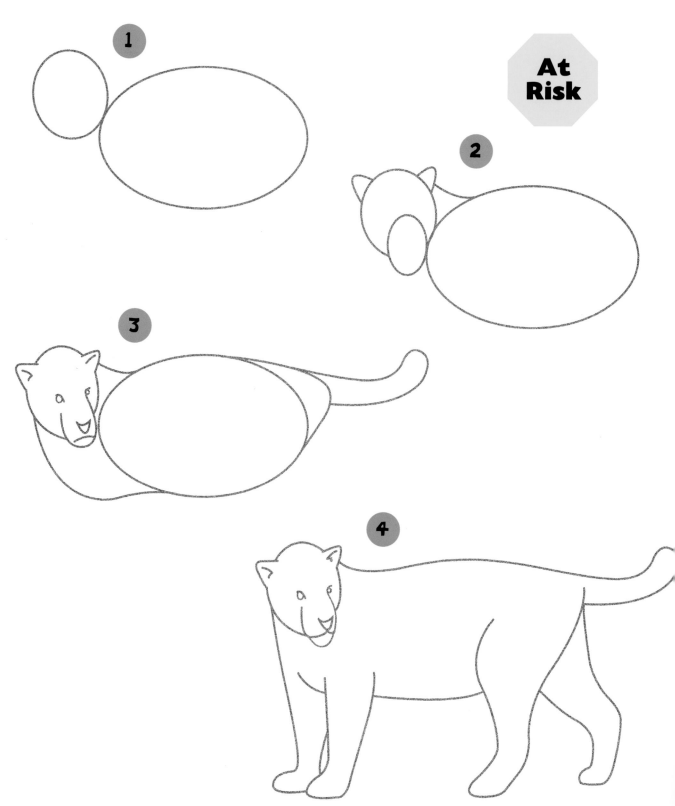

At Risk

5

At Risk

Jaguar **habitats**, or natural environments, are being destroyed by humans. With shrinking hunting grounds, some jaguars eat animals on ranches. Ranchers often catch and poison them. Some humans also hunt jaguars for their beautiful fur.

6

fun fact

Your housecat may hate the water, but jaguars are excellent swimmers! They love to play in rivers and streams. Jaguars mostly look for **prey**—or animals they can eat—on the ground, but they also hunt in the water. Sometimes, a jaguar may climb a tree to pounce on animals below.

Blue-Crowned Motmot

This colorful bird has a bright turquoise crown and red eyes. Its racket-shaped tail feathers swing back and forth.

fun fact

Instead of building nests up in trees, motmots dig long tunnels to nest in. "Motmot" is an American-Spanish word that sounds like the call these birds make.

Flying Fox

This furry flier is not a fox. It's a large fruit bat!
It has big, round eyes and wide wings.

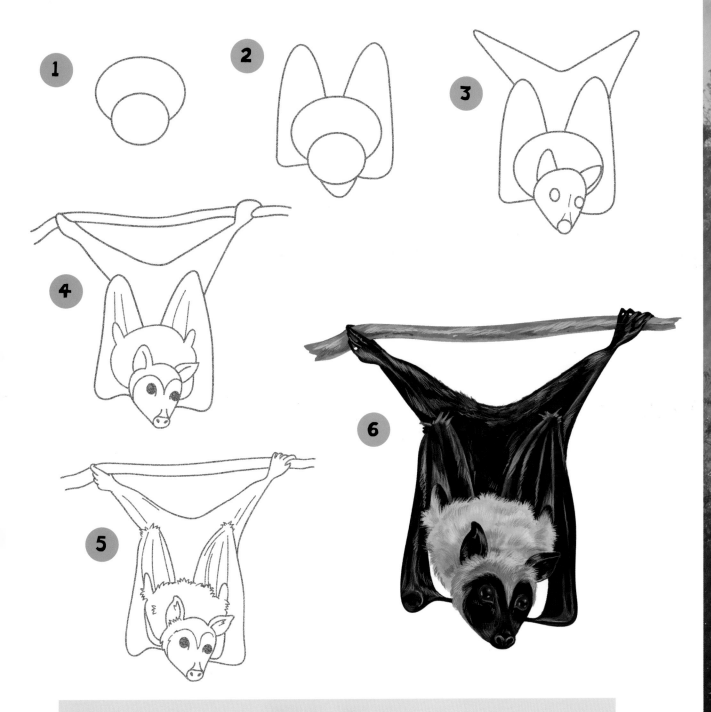

fun fact

All bats belong to the order *chiroptera*, which means "hand" and "wing" in Greek.
Their wings are actually long arms and fingers covered by a thin skin. Bats fly by
flapping their wings. They move their arms and fingers to dive and turn.

Crocodile

A crocodile is a large, spiny reptile with powerful jaws and super sharp teeth!

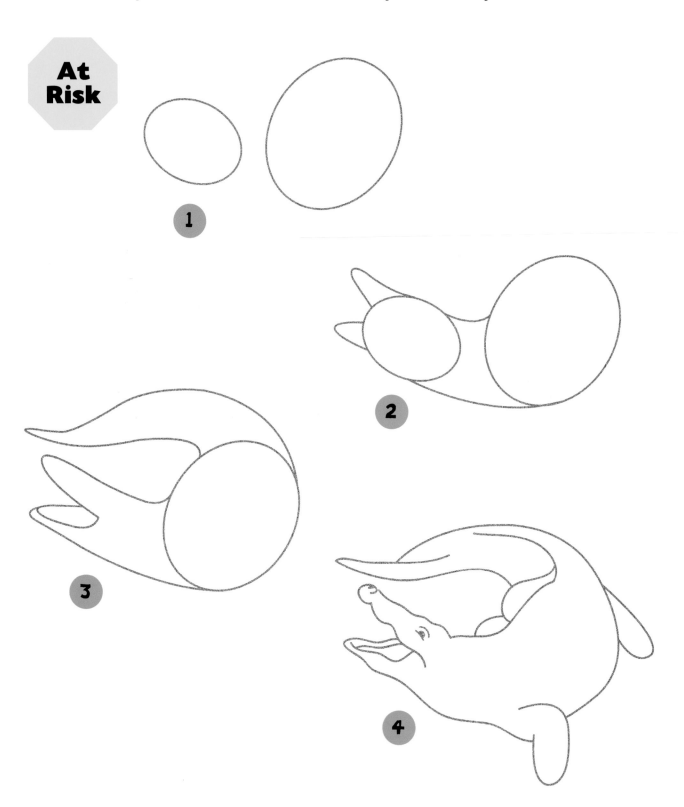

At Risk

1

2

3

4

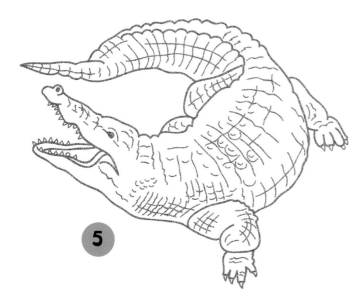

5

At Risk

Many crocodile species are endangered, because people hunt them for their skin to make shoes, wallets, and other things. Humans have also taken over their homes.

6

fun fact

You can tell the difference between crocodiles and alligators by looking at their jaws. Crocodiles have longer, thinner snouts than alligators. Crocodiles also have two long teeth on their lower jaws that stick up when their mouths are closed.

Toucan

This popular bird is known for its super-sized, rainbow-colored bill. The curved bill is great for getting food in hard-to-reach places!

At Risk

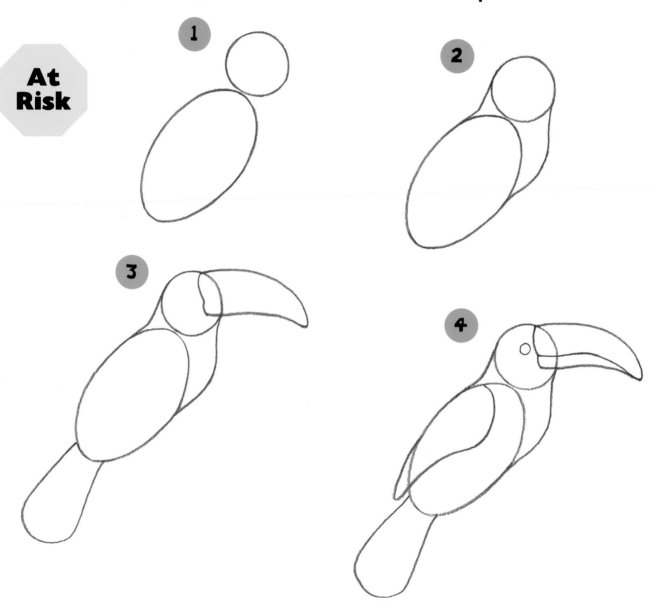

fun fact

The toucan's closest relative is the woodpecker. The two birds look very different, but they actually have a lot in common. Both move around on strong feet with two toes pointed backward and two pointed forward. They also have long, skinny, feather-like tongues.

5

6

7

At Risk

The rainforest is the keel-billed toucan's natural home. So the more rainforest land that is lost, the more at risk this bird becomes.

15

Howler Monkey

Howler monkeys are named for the loud calls they make.
They use their tails as a fifth hand.

fun fact

This monkey's howl can be heard up to three miles away! Howler monkeys call out at dawn and dusk to let other howlers know to stay away from their territory.

Capybara

The capybara looks like a furry pig with a beaver's face and webbed feet.

fun fact

The capybara is also called a "water pig," because it stays near the water, but it is actually a large rodent. Rodents are a group of small mammals that include guinea pigs, mice, and squirrels.

Amazon River Dolphin

The Amazon river dolphin is pink with a long, thin snout and small eyes.

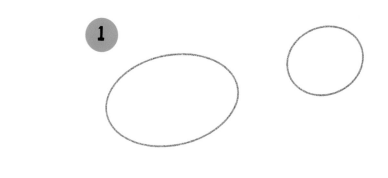

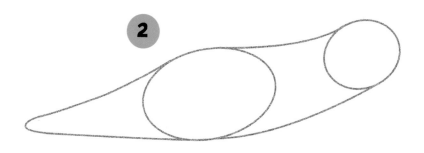

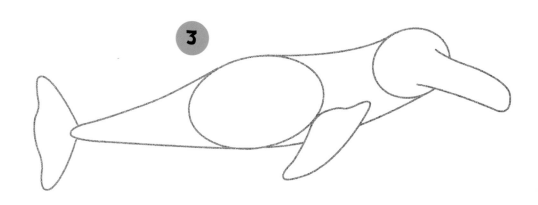

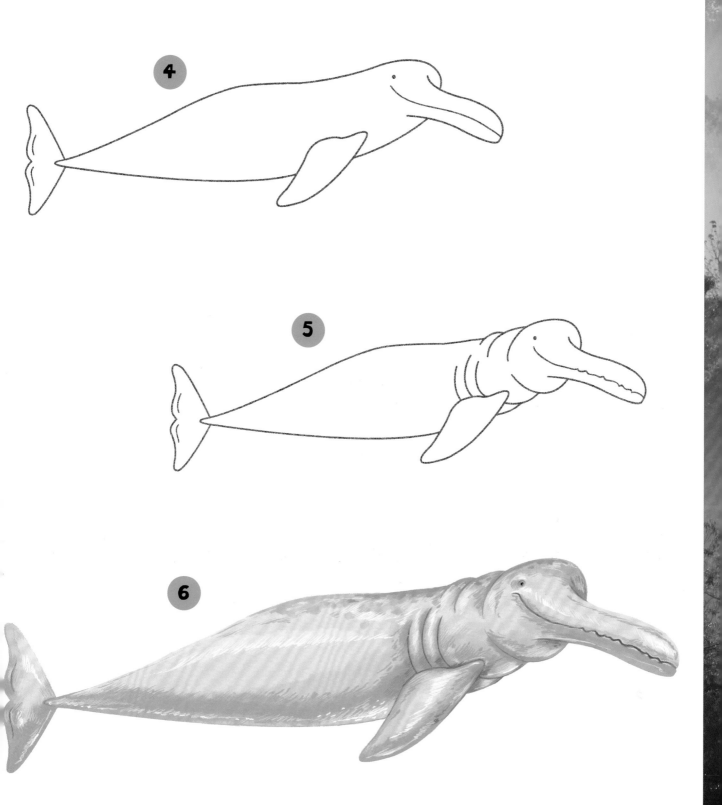

fun fact

When the Amazon River rises, river dolphins swim through the flooded rainforest floor. They can't see very well, but they find their way around with sonar. Sonar uses sound waves to locate things in the water.

Leopard

Leopards have dark spots on their fur. These markings help them blend into forests or grasslands.

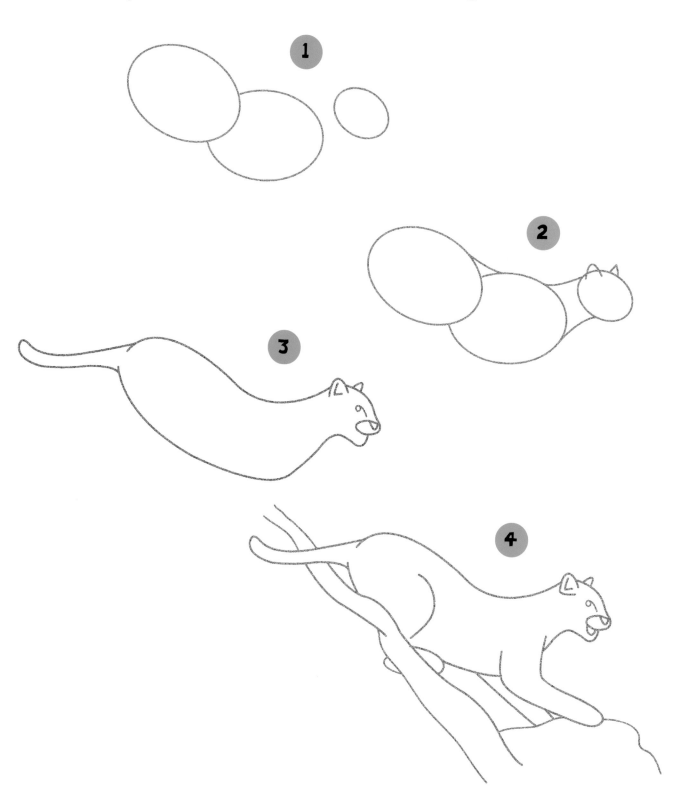

fun fact

It's easy to mix up the leopard and the jaguar, but a leopard has a
thinner body and face. It lives in Africa and Asia, whereas jaguars
are found in Mexico, Central America, and South America.

Orangutan

orangutan means "person of the forest" in Malay. This orange-haired ape spends most of its time swinging through forest treetops.

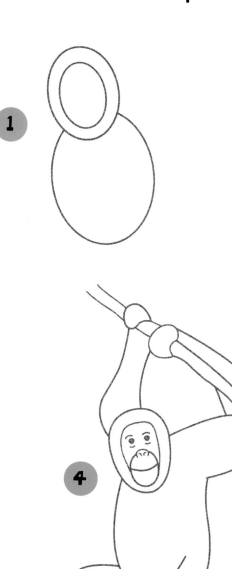

At Risk

Humans have destroyed most of the rainforests in Asia where orangutans live. Orangutan mothers are often killed and their young apes are illegally sold.

5

6

fun fact

Orangutans have a throat pouch that works like a microphone. It makes their voices very loud. Males, who enjoy spending time alone, have larger pouches than females. The calls they make to keep other orangutans from bothering them can be heard more than a mile away!

Forest Elephant

Elephants are the largest mammals on land.
These gray giants flap their huge ears to keep cool.

At Risk

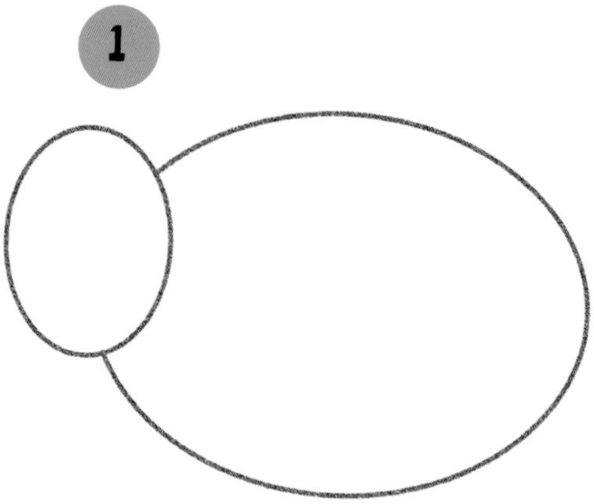

1

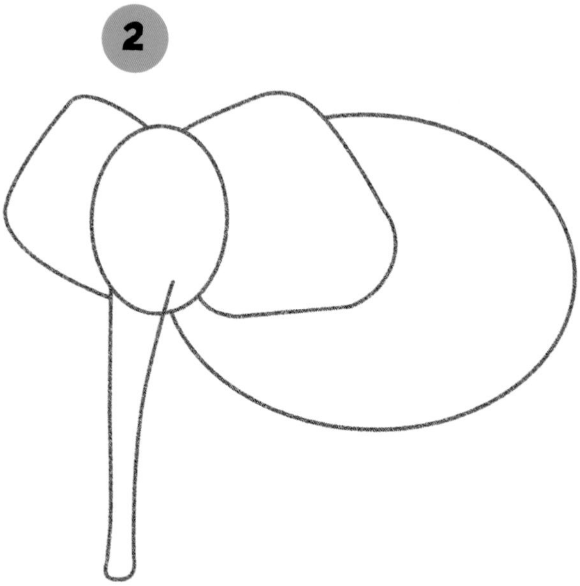

2

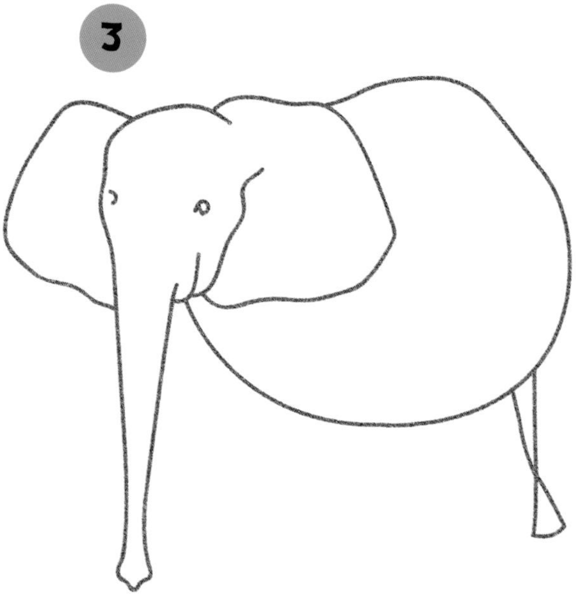

3

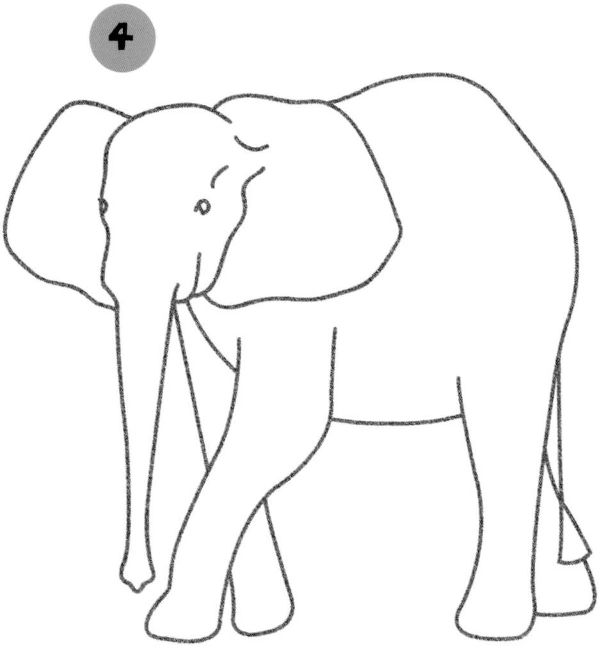

4

5

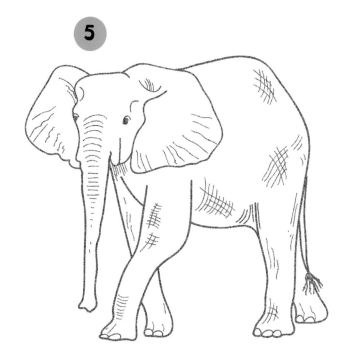

At Risk

Elephants are endangered. Before the ivory trade became illegal in the 1980s, many African elephants were hunted for their tusks. Also, loggers cut down the trees in the forest elephant's home and hunters kill these animals for their meat.

6

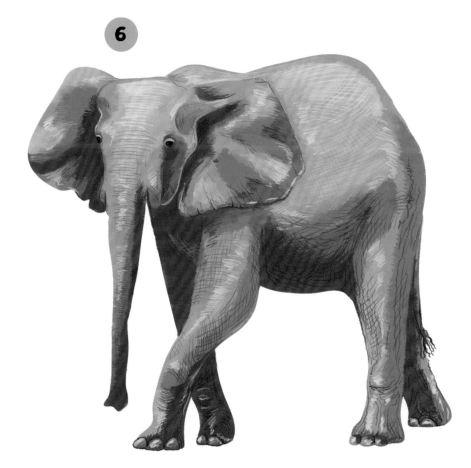

fun fact

An elephant's long trunk has thousands of different muscles used to smell, drink, grab food, and make sounds. It is like a nose, straw, hand, and trumpet all in one!

Sloth

A sloth spends most of its time upside down.
Its long, curved claws allow it to hang from trees.

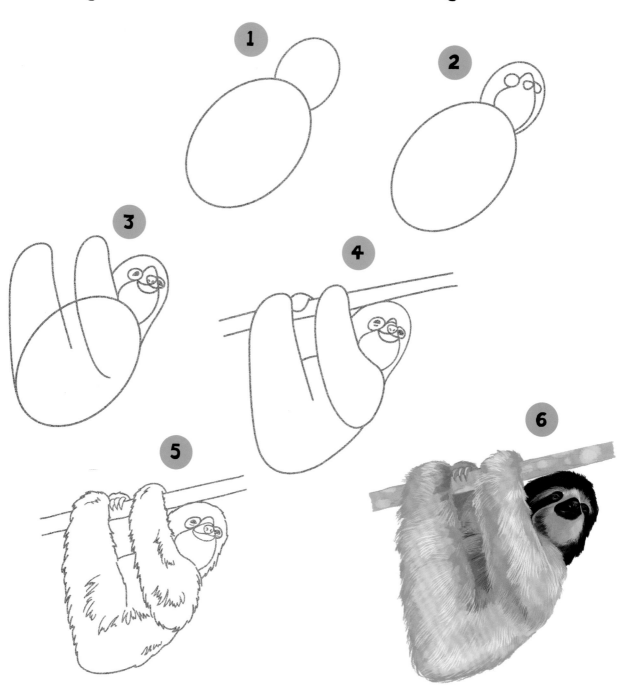

fun fact

"Sloth" means "laziness," which is a perfect way to describe the slowest-moving mammal in the world! Sloths sleep up to 20 hours a day. They stay still for so long that algae grows on their fur!

Iguana

An iguana is a scaly reptile with a spiny ridge along its back and a loose throat flap. The iguana's long tail makes up half its length!

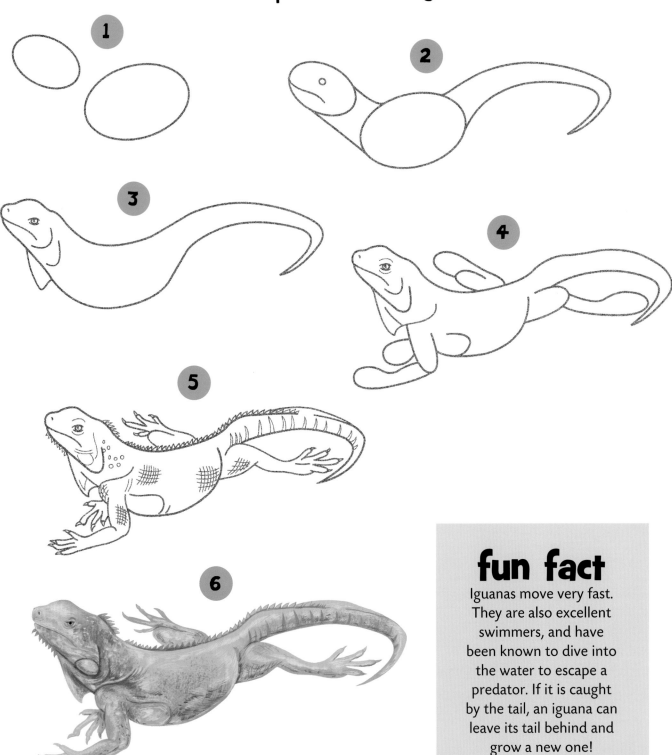

fun fact

Iguanas move very fast. They are also excellent swimmers, and have been known to dive into the water to escape a predator. If it is caught by the tail, an iguana can leave its tail behind and grow a new one!

Poison Dart Frog

This frog's bright colors let enemies know it is poisonous. Poison frogs can be red, orange, yellow, green, blue, or black.

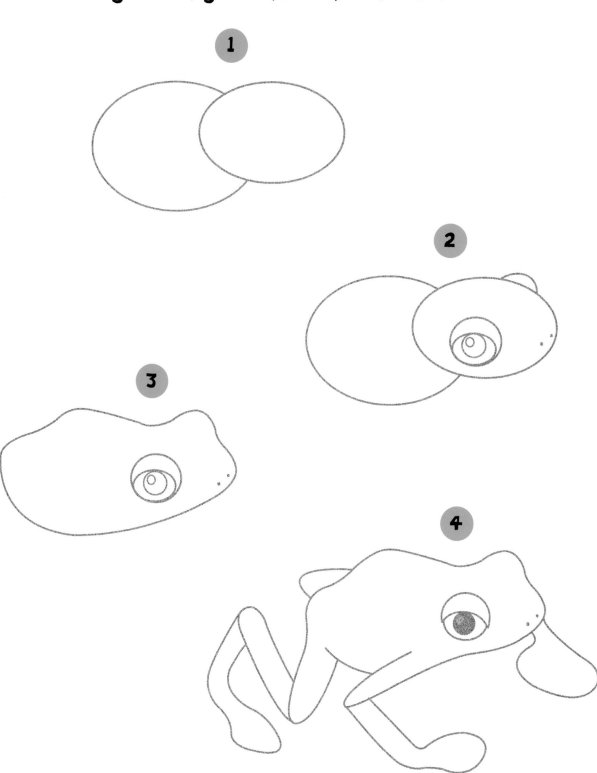

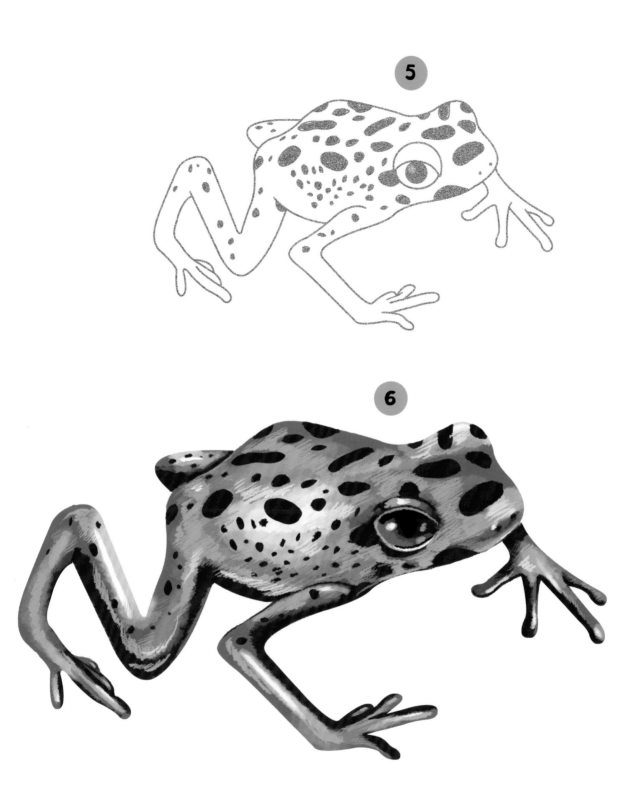

5

6

fun fact

Poison frogs eat poisonous insects and store the toxins in their colorful skin. They are called poison dart frogs because some Indian groups in South America tip their blow darts with the frog's poison.

Lorikeet

Lorikeets are one of the most colorful types of parrots. They have long, pointed tails and a brush-like tongue.

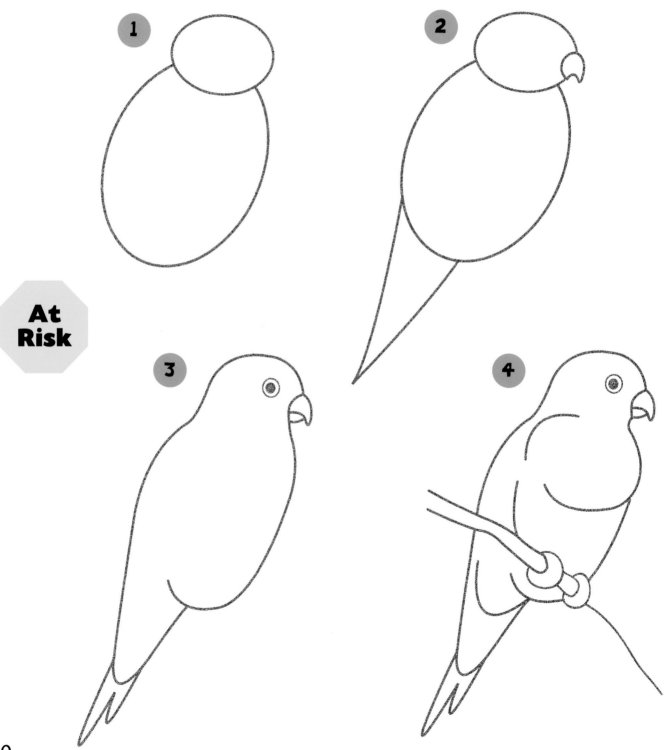

At Risk

5

6

At Risk

Humans pose a big threat to lorikeets. They kill these birds for their beautiful feathers or catch them to sell as pets.

fun fact

Lorikeets love to eat! They are also called "honeyeaters" because they snack on flowers, pollen, and nectar all day. To feed on hard-to-reach flowers, a lorikeet can hang upside down!

Anaconda

The common, or green, anaconda is the largest snake in the world. It can grow up to 30 feet long and weigh up to 550 pounds!

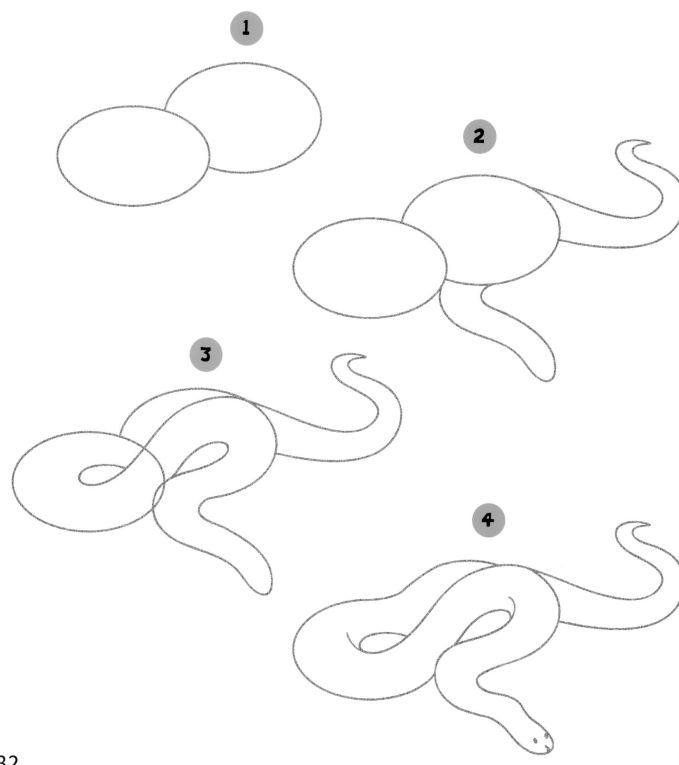

fun fact

Anacondas don't chew their food. They wrap their long bodies around prey and squeeze until the animal stops breathing. Then they swallow it whole—even animals as big as deer and jaguars! After a meal, an anaconda can go weeks or months without eating.

Scarlet Macaw

A scarlet macaw's bold red, blue, green, and yellow feathers help it blend in with the colorful fruits and flowers of the rainforest.

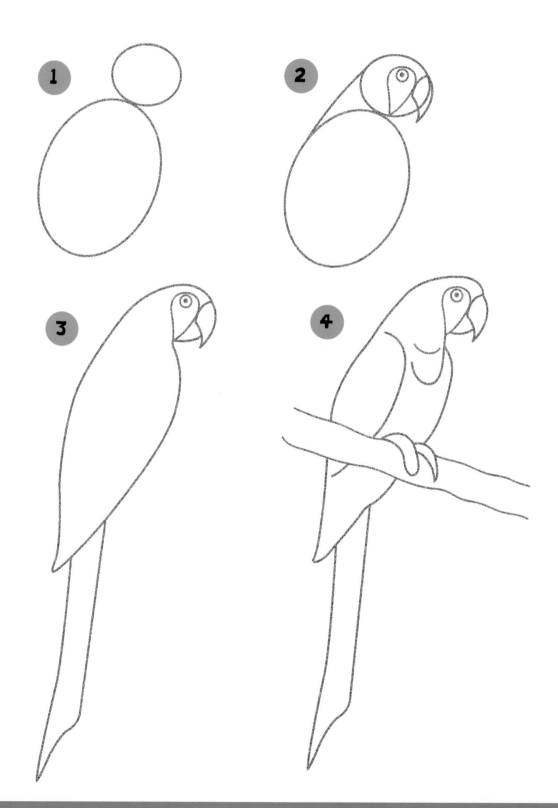

fun fact

Scarlet macaws are left-handed—or footed. They use their left
foot to hold things, while balancing on their right foot.

Sun Bear

The sun bear got its name from the curved mark on its chest that looks like the rising sun.

fun fact

The sun bear is the smallest bear in the world. It is also called the "dog bear" for its small size, light-colored muzzle, and muscular build. Sun bears have long tongues perfect for getting honey out of beehives, earning them their other nickname, "honey bears."

Baboon

Baboons have long noses and thick, frizzy fur.
Their rumps are totally bare!

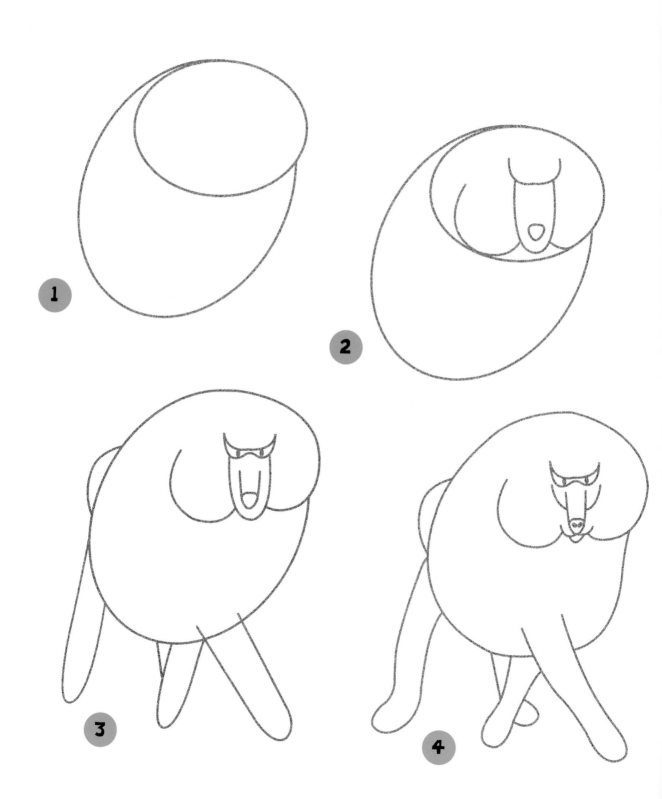

5

6

fun fact
Humans make different faces when we are happy, sad, or angry.
Baboons also make many faces! Each face sends other baboons a
message, such as "I'm sorry" or "stay away."

Piranha

This fearsome fish was named for its razor-sharp bite. "Piranha" combines the Portuguese words for "fish" and "tooth."

fun fact

Piranhas have a bad rap. In movies, they are shown as blood-thirsty monsters that eat people. However, there is no proof that a piranha has ever killed a person. Piranhas eat both plants and meat. They may feed on larger animals that have been hurt and have fallen into the water.

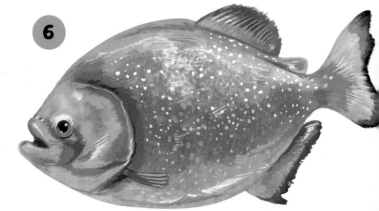